Rookie Read-About™ Science

Quack and Honk

By Allan Fowler

Consultants:

Robert L. Hillerich, Ph.D., Bowling Green
State University, Bowling Green, Ohio

Mary Nalbandian, Director of Science,
Chicago Public Schools, Chicago, Illinois

Fay Robinson, Child Development Specialist

CHILDRENS PRESS®

CHICAGO

Design by Beth Herman Design Associates

Library of Congress Cataloging-in-Publication Data

Fowler, Allan
    Quack and honk / by Allan Fowler.
        p. cm. –(Rookie read-about science)
    Summary: Briefly describes the physical characteristics and habits
of ducks and geese.
    ISBN 0-516-06012-0
    1. Anatidae–Juvenile literature. [1. Ducks. 2. Geese]
  I. Title. II. Series: Fowler, Allan. Rookie read-about science.
QL696.A52F69 1993
598.4'1–dc20   92-35056
                                                            CIP
                                                            AC

Have you ever gone
swimming with rubber
fins on your feet?

They help you push
against the water – and
make it easier to swim.

Ducks and geese have
webbed feet, which work
like swim fins.

So ducks and geese are
great swimmers.

Of course, they also
waddle around on land.

And they can fly very
far and very fast.

Geese and ducks are
known as waterfowl.

Domestic ducks and geese
live on poultry farms.

Wild ducks and geese live
on ponds, or in marshes,
or along streams or the
ocean shore.

There are many kinds of
wild geese and ducks.

11

A male duck is called a
drake. Drakes often have
brightly colored feathers.

Female ducks are usually brown.

Baby ducks are called ducklings. These ducklings have just hatched from eggs.

15

A male goose is called
a gander.

And baby geese are
called goslings.

Ducks have wider, flatter
bills than geese.

Geese are usually bigger
than ducks.

Geese honk and ducks quack.

In winter, ducks and geese can't find insects, seeds, and other things they eat.

So every fall wild ducks and geese fly south. They spend the winter where the weather is warm and there is plenty of food.

Then in the spring they
fly back to their homes
in the north.

We say that birds migrate
when they make these
long flights.

Ducks and geese usually
fly in a V-shaped
formation, like this flock
of snow geese.

Domestic geese and ducks don't migrate. The farmers make sure they have enough to eat all year round.

How do migrating ducks
and geese find their way?

Nobody knows for sure –
except the ducks and the
geese.

And if you ask them,
all they will say is quack
or honk.

29

Words You Know

waterfowl

ducks

geese

webbed feet

duck　　　　bill

drake

duckling

gander

goslings

V-shaped formation

31

Index

About the Author

Allan Fowler is a free-lance writer with a background in advertising. Born in New York, he lives in Chicago now and enjoys traveling.

Photo Credits

Grant Heilman Photography, Inc. – ©Thomas Hovland, Cover, 29

PhotoEdit – ©David Young-Wolff, 14, 19, 30 (top right)

SuperStock International, Inc. – ©BL Productions, 3; ©Alan Briere, 7 ; ©Stanley Johnson, 18, 30 (bottom right); ©David Corson, 22; ©Herbert Crossan, 25; ©John Warden, 26, 30 (top left), 31 (bottom); ©Tom Rosenthal, 27

Valan – ©Kennon Cooke, 5, 12, 31 (top left); ©Jean Bruneau, 8; ©Val & Alan Wilkinson, 9, 10 (left); ©Arthur Christiansen, 10 (right); ©Wayne Lankinen, 11 (top left and top right), 17, 31 (center right); ©Jeff Foott, 11 (bottom left); ©Albert Kuhnigk, 11 (bottom right); ©S.J. Krasemann, 16, 31 (center left); ©Dennis W. Schmidt, 21; ©Pam Hickman, 30 (bottom left)

VIREO – ©D. Roby/K. Brink, 13

Visuals Unlimited – ©William J. Weber, 15, 31 (top right)

COVER: Embden Geese, Roven and Pekin ducks